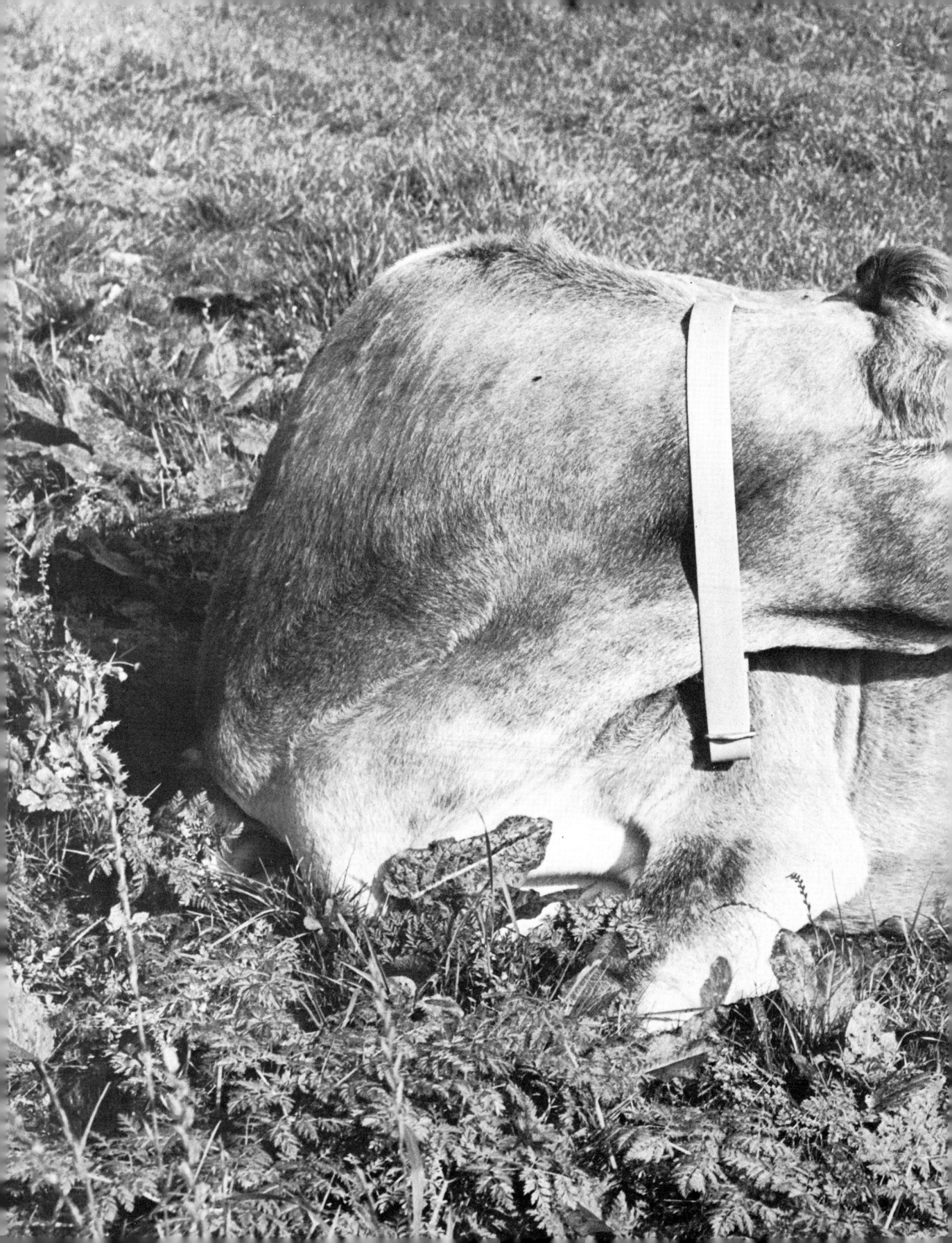

A Calf is Born

Jane Miller

J. M. Dent & Sons Ltd
London Toronto Melbourne

First published 1981
© Jane Miller 1981

Designed by Malcolm Young
Phototypeset in VIP Century Schoolbook by
Trident Graphics Limited, Reigate
Printed and bound in Singapore
by Tien Wah Press (PTE) Ltd
for J. M. Dent & Sons Ltd
Aldine House, Welbeck Street, London

The author and publishers are grateful
for the help of Major J. A. Pelly, D.L., J.P.,
Preshaw Estate, Upham, Hampshire,
and of Peter Lewis, Herdsman of Preshaw Herd
of Pedigree Jersey Cattle,
and of Hazel Underwood, Calf-Rearer.

British Library Cataloguing in Publication Data

Miller, Jane
    A calf is born.
    1. Calves – Pictorial works – Juvenile literature
    I. Title
636.2'07   SF205

ISBN 0–460–06986–1

This is a Jersey calf. It is only one day old.

The calf's father is a Jersey bull.

These Jersey cows will soon give birth to calves.

One of them is looking for a quiet place
to have her calf.

She lies down ready to give birth.

The calf has been growing in the cow's belly
for 284 days – 9½ months – protected by a water-bag.
The water-bag comes out first.

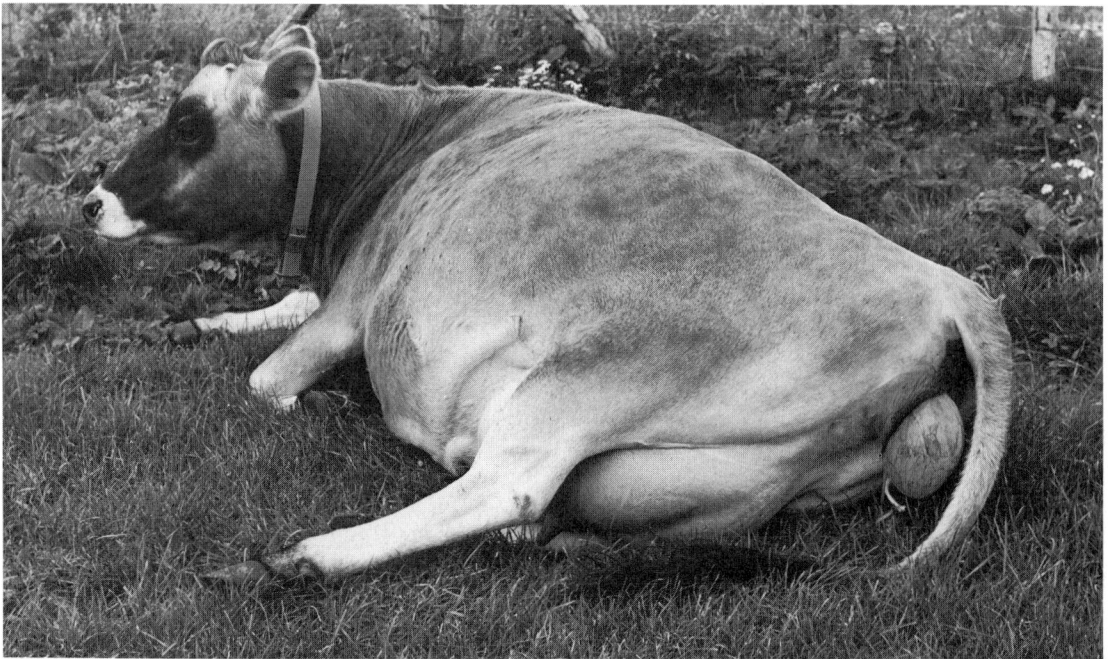

It breaks so that the calf can get out.

Within a few minutes the calf is born.
It is still wet from the birth and is attached
to its mother by the umbilical cord.
The cord carried the mother's food
to the calf while it was in her belly.

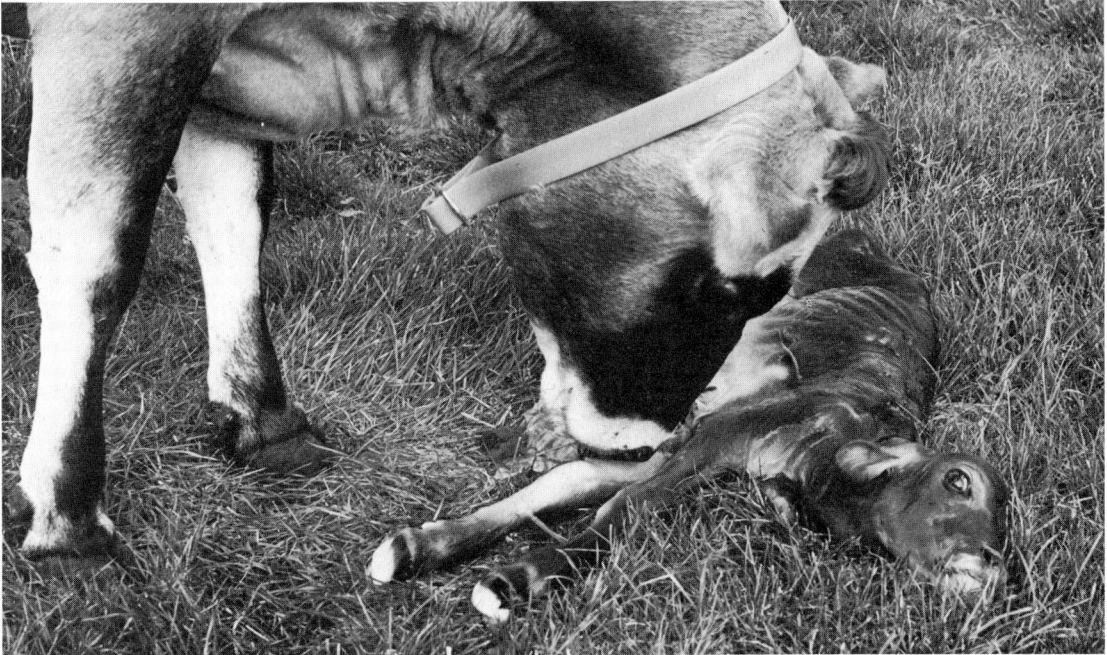

As the cow stands up the cord breaks.
She smells her calf and licks it clean.

It is a heifer,
a female calf.
The calf soon
begins to recognize
its mother.

It tries to get up
but is still so weak
that it falls down
several times.
Finally it manages
to stand by itself.

The calf is hungry.
The cow helps it
to find her udder
which is full of milk
so that the calf
can drink.

The cow stays
beside her calf
for the rest
of the day.

Late that afternoon Hazel,
the girl who looks after the calves,
takes them to join the other cows
and calves in the barn.

On this farm every calf spends
the first five nights with its mother
so that it can drink her rich milk.

The calves are now ready to leave their mothers.
The bull calves are taken to market to be sold.
The heifer calves are reared in calf pens.

The mother cows return to the herd
and are milked twice a day by machine.

Their milk is taken daily by lorry
to a factory where it is bottled.
Then it is sold to people to drink.

Hazel is preparing
dried milk to feed
to the heifer calves.

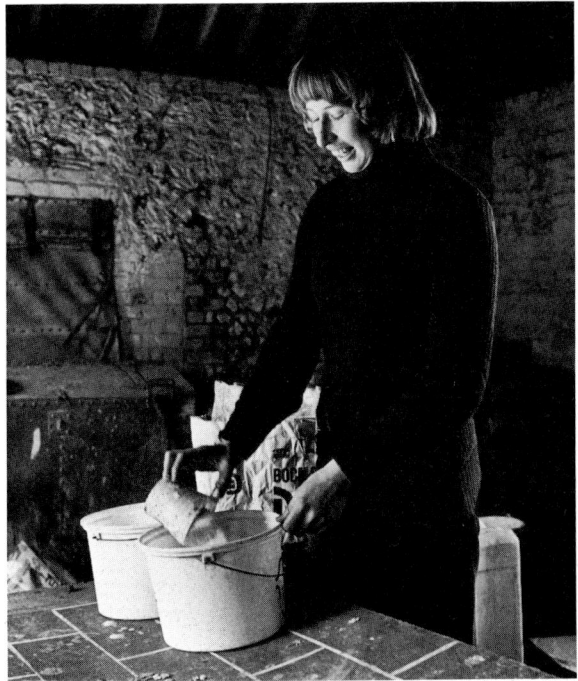

Then she carries it
to the calf pens.

The farm collie follows Hazel everywhere.

At first
the young calves
are taught to suck
the milk
through a teat
on a bottle.

This calf is sick
and needs special care.
Hazel feeds it from
a bottle and keeps it
in a pen heated by
an infra-red lamp.

The next day,
by holding the teat
in their mouths,
Hazel teaches them
to suck the milk
straight from the
bucket.

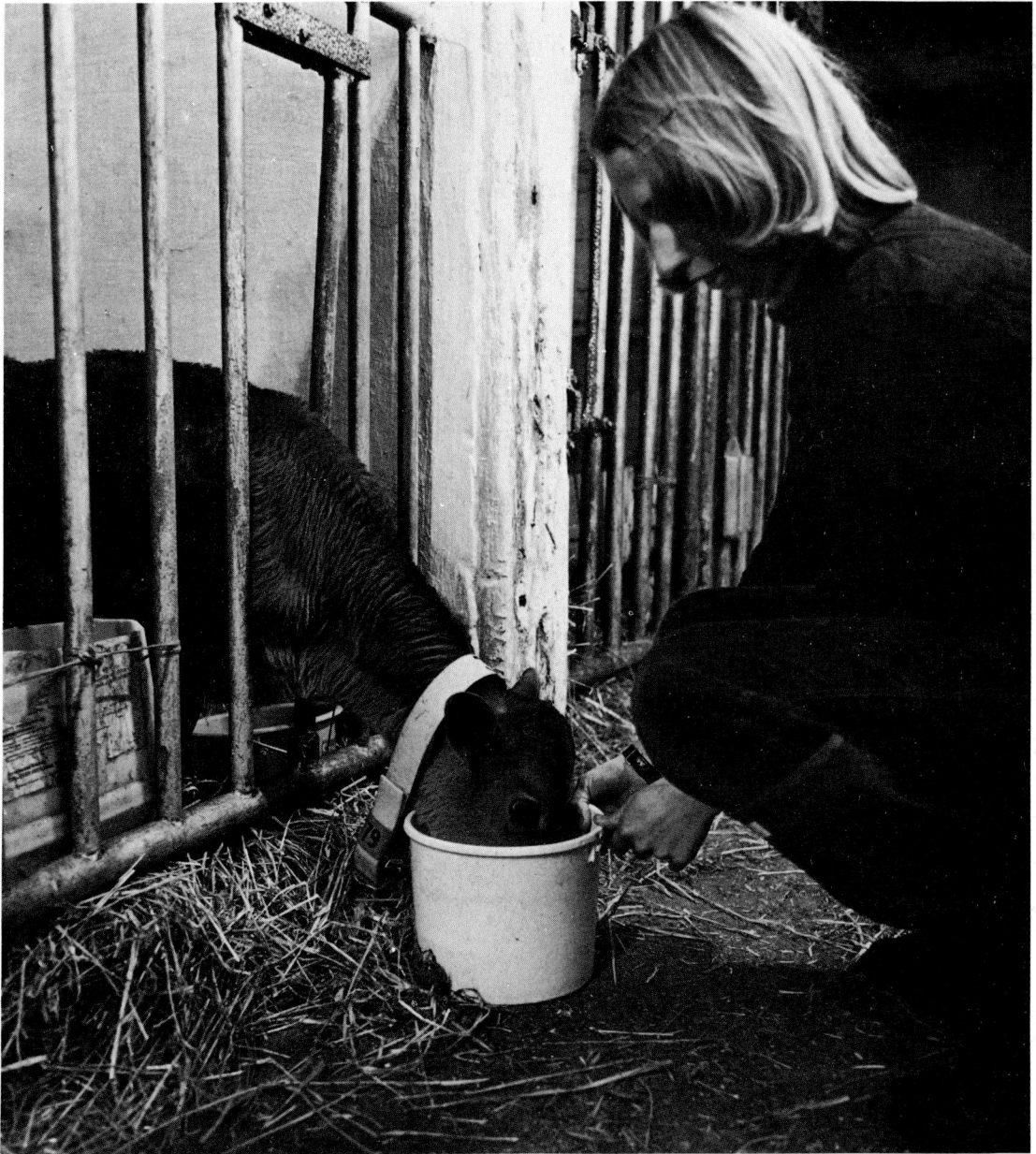

Hazel makes sure the calves are drinking properly.

The calves enjoy
their milk.
So does the collie
which licks the
buckets when
the calves have
finished drinking.

All calves are given
small weaning nuts
to nibble.

This helps them
become used to
solid food.
The nuts are put in
boxes in their pens
as soon as they
are weaned from
their mothers.

As they grow older the calves also learn to eat
from the nets full of hay that are hung in their pens.

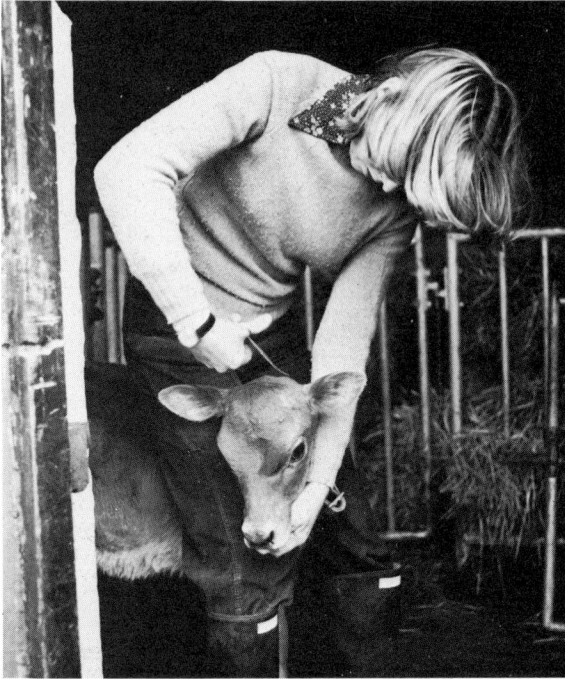

All calves have their horns removed in the first few weeks. After clipping away the hair, the tiny horns are singed off.

They are given injections so that they do not feel any pain.

Each calf must have
a number marked
inside one ear
with a coloured dye;
it is called
an "ear number".

This does not hurt
the calf either.

When they are five weeks old the calves are weaned
from drinking milk and eat only nuts and hay.
After three to four months
they move from the calf pens to the barn.

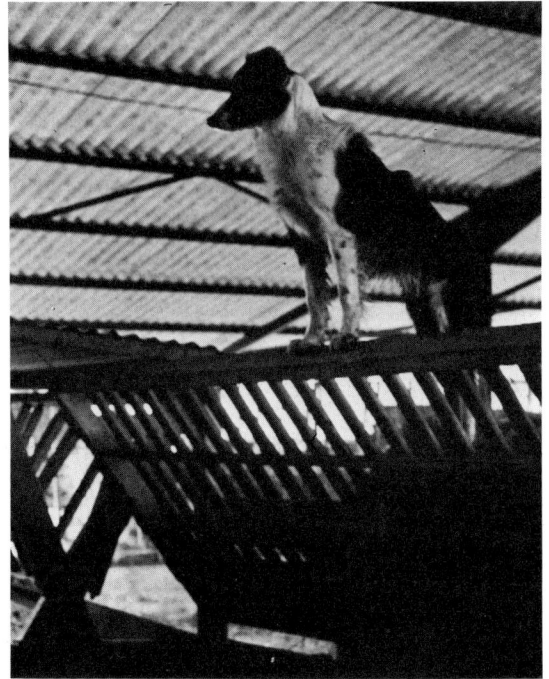

The calves live in the barn
until they are six to eight months old.
When the weather is warmer
they are taken out to live in the fields where
Hazel continues to feed them cattle-nuts and hay.

The calves now feed together from troughs.
The farm collie waits anxiously
to see if they will leave any food for her.

When they are
two years old
it will be their turn
to be mothers.
Then they will have
their first calves
and become
milking cows.

In the spring sunshine
they race
around the field
enjoying their freedom.

Many different kinds of food are made from milk — cream, butter and cheese are some of them.